A Taste of Salt

A Taste of Salt

Poems

To Kristen
Teacher - Advisor -
Friend - Thank you
so much -
Mary Katherine
November 2018

Mary Katherine Wainwright

Editor Judyth Hill; book cover and book design Mary Meade.

A Taste of Salt is available on Amazon.com

A Taste of Salt/Mary Katherine Wainwright. —1st ed.

ISBN 978-1727336023

To my children

Kathy, Angela, Georgia, GJohn

with overflowing love and pride

and to the memory of The Aunts

Contents

Acknowledgements

Thanks to the following publications in which these poems first appeared: *Florida English, Harp Strings Poetry Journal, Kalliope, Phoebe, Red Raven Review, Sarasota Review, Song of the Siren, White Pelican Review*

My many teachers and readers have always appeared right on time. With much gratitude for their expertise and generosity of spirit, for thoughtful readings and suggestions: Sandra Cisneros, Judyth Hill, Kristen Iversen, Jon Looney, Donna Masini, Mary Meade, William Slaughter, Kathy Snodgrass.

I am also indebted to the National Endowment for the Humanities; the Florida Endowment Fund for Higher Education; the Writer's Voice—New York, Siena, Tampa; the Seaside/FIU Writers' Workshop; the University of New Orleans Creative Writing Low Residency Workshop; the Paris Writers' Workshop; the Spoleto Writers' Workshop.

Preface

Language, for Mary Katherine Wainwright, is a way of knowing and feeling the world—and a way of remembering and recording. What she has given us, here, is a book of moments and essences, weighted by gravity and elevated by grace.

Wainwright's poems are at once familiar and strange. They collect themselves like photographs in a family album and, at the same time, read like handwritten notes in a secret diary. Can poems give their secrets away and keep them too? Reading Wainwright's poems has me believing they can.

Longing and fulfillment are the poles of this book, and of the poems in it, and like the earth's poles they come fully charged with their magnets on.

"It was my own voice I heard—soft," Wainwright whispers, "speaking from scars carved like lace under the skin." See the scars and notice the fineness of the carving, but whatever else you do with the poems in *A Taste of Salt*, listen hard for *that* voice. And when you hear it, let yourself go . . . everywhere it takes you.

—William Slaughter
Author: *Untold Stories* and *The Politics of My Heart*
Editor: *Mudlark, An Electronic Journal of Poetry and Poetics*

Foreword

A Taste of Salt, Mary Katherine Wainwright's long awaited first published volume of poetry, is about the beat of fleeting Time, the palpable presence of absence, and the sugar and salt of our deepest longings.

For nearly ten years, Wainwright has been active in the literary life and goings-on south of the border in beautiful San Miguel de Allende, Mexico. Reading her poetry, you retrace her adventures ranging from New York City, to Spain, France, Italy, and Greece. And you will also be treated to her indelible memories of growing up in her North Florida. You'll meet the family: her mother, grandmother, father, Uncle Frank, the Aunts, and long ago loves.

Throughout *A Taste of Salt*, Wainwright's poetry is marked by a precision and economy of language. She demonstrates for her readers the power and necessity of memory and the act of remembering. She weaves a tapestry of images, feelings, and places, sees connections and seeks parallels between her personal near-present and ancient classical mythology. Be prepared for some unexpected and powerful juxtapositions of phrase, such as "they buried the dead and planted potatoes," and "The past is a yellow buttercup under your chin." Lines such as these only come from the heart, and pen, of a fine poet.

—Jon R. Looney
Author: *Bluffwalker, Snakedoctor, Whistlepig*.

Time held me green and dying/ though I sang in my chains like the sea.

—Dylan Thomas

Saudade is a Portuguese expression that is almost untranslatable.
The best way to describe it is:
the presence of absence.
It is a longing for someone or something
that you remember fondly
but know you can never experience again.

a world unsuspected/ beckons to new places/ and no whiteness (lost) is so white as the memory/ of whiteness.

—William Carlos Williams

Essences

When I could stand the turmoil no more, I closed the door.
Dark settled outside the window. Even the cats curled up. Snow
piled high, but a yellow Crocus broke through. Finally, it was
my own voice I heard—soft, speaking from scars carved like lace
under the skin.

The Last Southern Daughter *(after Charles Simic)*

1

I am the last southern daughter. I have much work to do. Each day I iron organdy pinafores and polish white Mary Jane slippers. Other daughters no longer call on me. Their dresses gather dust. Shoes pile up on the floor while they wear plaid shirts and march west in a straight line. The sun shines only on me. I carry my umbrella to protect my skin from freckles.

2

I am the last southern daughter. At the piano recital I play *Glow Worm* and *Spinning Song*. My uncle praises my rhythm. My aunt admires my green gown. When I curtsy, my mother says, *Mind your manners. Your father has run away with the delivery boy, and we need to buy bread for supper.*

3

I am the last southern daughter. My grandmother sits in the closet under the stairs.   She wraps newspapers under her blouse to keep warm and reads romance novels by the light of a single hanging light bulb. My mother and aunt play solitaire every afternoon from twelve until four o'clock. They keep score. The neighbors think they are napping. They think my grandmother is a changeling.

Memorabilia

Does he remember the note she wrote
that drizzling November evening, 1939?

Can he still picture her
at the worn desk facing the second-floor window
of Uncle Frank's old farm house?
Perhaps she wore a satin robe
    later folded in tissue and left
    in the cedar chest at the top of the stairs.

Perhaps her brown hair was swinging loose
as she rested her chin in her hand,
stared out at leafless pecan trees
and wrote on pale blue paper
the words I found last week:

    My dearest, Tomorrow
    please don't forget to kiss me.
    Right after you put the ring on
    is when you're supposed to kiss me.

Beneath baskets of golden mums
she turned and walked into forty years.

Rice

for Joy Harjo

Tonight the smell of rice
reminds me of my mother
standing at the stove in a dress and heels

while I sit on a kitchen stool watching her
cook rice with fried chicken on Sundays,
beef stew in winter,
fresh fish caught in some hidden lake near that small north-
    Florida town,
sometimes rice on Fridays in October when I'm happy
as the sunset blends deep into autumn darkness,
mingles with the smell of wood burning in the chimney smoke.

My age doesn't matter.
My mother always cooked rice for us and my father.

In a few minutes
we will hear his truck in the driveway.
The kitchen door will open and he will come in.
Is he angry? Or playful and telling stories?

We don't know yet, but when he comes in
whatever is happening between my mother and me
will be broken.

Forty years later I stand in my own kitchen cooking rice for me
     alone.
The room is still.
The only sound is slowly boiling rice.

My mother comes here too,
watches with me.

For a moment we look at each other across the years
as if he hadn't come through the door,
as if I hadn't grown up,
as if we could reach across.

The Annunciation *(after Sharon Olds)*

   At the center of some Renaissance painting
the angel kneels beside a fluted marble column.
Black cypress trees, rigid as Roman armies,
line up behind his head. He offers a white lily.
Mary sits in her blue robe, her hands folded,
a halo crowning her head,
her book still open, abandoned on the floor.
The dove hovers overhead.
They are about to enact the scene.
The angel is about to reveal the mystery.
Mary is about to acquiesce. She is young. She is pregnant.
She only knows she has no choice.
She has not been asked.

   I want to go to her and say—No. Tell them No.
Refuse the angel—you are the wrong woman.
This is the wrong act; terrible things will happen.
You cannot imagine. You will suffer in ways you never thought of.
I want to go to her there on her throne that April afternoon
and say it, her astonished eyes turning to me
as I urge her to retrieve her book,
become a scholar, a philosopher, a poet,
change the course of history, the destiny of women.
I want to say
the world will not learn from your sacrifice.
But I don't. The heavenly host gathered in the corner
drown out my voice.

Easter Sunday

We took flowers to the cemetery, my father and I, pots of white lilies for relatives, one pink rose for mother. I can see him still, 89 years old, plaid suspenders holding up baggy trousers, his cane guiding him along crumbling brick paths through rusted iron gates as he passed each grave, telling me stories of our family: my great grandfather sheriff, killed in pursuit of an escaped convict; James, the baby who died too soon. They were all there that day, more alive to him than I was. We paused and sat quietly by a border of deep green sago palms, watched a hawk chase a red-winged blackbird through the afternoon sky. Reluctant to leave, my father was making himself at home.

A Visit to St. Vincent's

The heavy breathing in the next room
fills the hallway.
The boy will not live, but that will come later.

I wait by my father's bed.
He sleeps. His yellowed body twitches.

Sometimes he speaks—incoherent words that wake him.
   I was dreaming, he says,
then reaches for a forbidden box of chocolates,
casting a defiant look at me, his oldest daughter.

In his sleep, his hands twist a lock of white hair on his forehead,
a familiar gesture. They reach through the air,
perhaps to tighten an imaginary line through the loops
of an imaginary fishing rod. He's fourteen again.
A different hot August sun beats down on a still lake of his youth.
The trout ignore his bait, circle the row boat.

The family gathers next door. They talk in whispers.
The boy's labored sounds are slower but just as heavy.

We don't speak, my father and I.
So much to say, yet nothing.

I look out the window
of this hospital where I was born,
watch the sun make its inevitable westward way.

My Aunt Ruth

moved through life in cotton flowered dresses with lace collars.
She made deviled eggs and pimento cheese
on hot summer afternoons in Miami.

In her flower shop, a detached garage behind the house,
she mixed glads and carns and statice, tall arrangements
my uncle delivered in his old car with the running board.

I became their child each summer
arriving on the *Silver Meteor.*
We went to the Miami Public Library

for the stack of novels forbidden at home—
no *Wind in the Willows* this summer—
then a miniature golf course on Coral Way

and afterward a foamy root beer float
at the pharmacy
with the marble-countered soda fountain.

She made my first cup of coffee milk,
served ice cream in ginger ale
when I had the mumps,

sewed new clothes when I went to college,
mailed tins of dates stuffed with pecans
and sprinkled with powdered sugar,

created an orange blossom bouquet for my wedding.
On my last visit she had closed the shutters
on the tall arched windows in the living room,

spread sheets over the peach damask sofa,
moved Tweetie Bird and Pete's old canary cages
to the garage, packed away the violet-painted china

and lived in the back bedroom
freezing home-made tv dinners
from her leftovers. She wanted to play canasta.

When we returned to the house after her funeral
we found the cedar chest upstairs
filled with embroidered baby clothes—

hats, dresses, little coats,
all covered with small pink flowers
carefully folded in white tissue paper.

The Cut Glass Bowl

always stood on the marble-top table
in the hall under the gilt mirror.
Tiny diamonds and crescents carved into the glass
made it sparkle, yet rough to touch.

My mother filled it with roses,
red and peach from her garden.
Their fragrance filled the hallway
as we came home each afternoon.

She bought it in New Orleans on her honeymoon,
chose it from the many bowls crowding oak shelves
at the antique dealer on Royal Street,
carried it back to the only home she would know:

my father's father's house on Clark Street—
white clap boards, screened porches, rocking chairs—
home to bridge parties on sunny afternoons,
Sunday dinners with fried chicken and mint tea.

When the bowl became mine, I rested it on a window ledge
on Stuyvesant Square in New York.
There it sat gleaming
through lace-curtained windows

where young sailors on their way
from the Fulton Street piers
could glimpse it in the candle light.
Did they see it and think of home?

Other times,
I filled it with punch for my children's parties.
Once I sat it beside a bathtub in a city apartment
to float brightly lit candles and drops of lavender oil.

The bowl is now on the piano.
Each tiny cut of glass still sparkles
as the sun sets through the western windows
and I watch for the first glimpse of Venus, the evening star.

On Old 301

to Papa

In the photograph he stands by the fence
wearing a straw hat, carrying his cane,
his suspenders sliding down stooped shoulders.

Behind him, the sweet peas bloom.
They came early that year,
slender green stems, pink blossoms

climbing on strings
he had so carefully tacked to the wooden frame
against the tin wall of the back shed.

To me, a child of five, tagging along behind,
it was as if the first mover moved again
along garden paths as I watched him

stop to pull a weed, clip a dead bud.
Even today, when I hear the buzz of dragonflies
I remember how the sun turned the hedge of Queen Anne's lace

into a sea of crystals
while in the background, all along Old 30l,
the cars kept their steady pace.

The Aunts

gathered on the porch of our old lake house,
    talked jazz tunes and lullabies.

There on the edge,
    we caught their notes, danced

in the circles of their words.
    Women with dreams

woven into the lives of their children
    sent us spinning into our own lives.

Their music trailing behind, rising within, around us.
    We clapped our hands,

tip-toed around their fullness.
    I have their smiles, dark hair, eyes.

On the days the Aunts gathered, we were all together
    and somehow it was always July.

Mad Women

For Eurydice,
all it took was a flick of a snake's tongue
to hurl her into darkness
and for Persephone, one small bite of fruit.

In my family, the women
don't need snakes or pomegranates
to start their descent.
They simply go mad when they turn fifty.

My grandmother sat herself down
in her rocker on the back porch,
stared at the chickens and tomato plants,
rocked, shelled peas, muttered curses at lizards.

My mother turned off the stove,
walked out of the kitchen,
lived on Coca-Cola in small bottles and Hershey's Kisses,
laid out endless games of solitaire.

As for me,
it begins with a taste of salt.
A tear that rolls into the corner of my mouth,
beads of sweat that gather in the hollow of a shoulder,

a sharp gust of sea spray on my face
are sufficient
to send me out into the night
in search of burning caves or a bottomless spring.

Last week at my daughter's wedding
I could only nod when she said to me
>   *My life will be the color of kale:*
>   *bright purple with ruffled green edges.*

A Mirage

It was the kind of day
when the sun danced on the tips of waves.
He passed me on the bridge
playing laughing games with the wind,
flashing a smile that said—come with me.

He gave me
a small painted heart hung on a black velvet ribbon
because, he said, every woman should have
a small painted heart on a black velvet ribbon
and chocolate doughnuts on rainy midnights
when the oak outside my window
made creaking sounds in the dark,

a poem he had read in a book
because he couldn't write the one
he carried inside himself,
days of sand and beer on the beach,
nights of soft guitar sounds and smoldering fires.

And I wonder still—on these days
when the sun dances on the tips of the waves—why
I took the exit and went my way alone.

Among the Islands

Old Greek sailors often dream with open eyes.

Seas fall yet small islands remain,
white buildings float in blue waves,
alleys lead to cobblestone paths.

By golden rocks we search ruins
listening for faint notes from Pan's pipe.
We follow the sun

and stir ancient dust looking for lost land,
find red Geraniums under white-washed windows,
steep stairs.

We go on, we seek, we dream—
wanderers afoot
here in the land of open eyes.

Anna Maria Island

1

For the sea, praise *moon-snail, coquina, banded tulip*
and for the night sky *Orion, the Big Dipper, Arcturus*
Here on the shore my bare feet leave no prints in the sand.

2

Some days I reach only for skeletons. Broken
outer shells expose spirals of smooth pink curves
delicate as Ionian columns or the leaves of the sea rose.
I take them home to bleach white in the sun.
This morning I pass a crusted, crab trap,
an oddity washed up from last night's storm,
watch a dolphin leap through the waves.

3

These days hurt my eyes with their fullness—
empty beaches late afternoons,
a solitary jogger moving to the rhythm of the waves,
a sailboat on the edge of the horizon.
Fog creeps in, covering the sails and our faces in gray mist.
At the beach café we two share a bowl of melon.

4

Last week an apple rolled in the surf,
bobbing in the seaweed beside a chipped whelk.
I thought perhaps
it must have traveled centuries from the Aegean
to lie there in the waves at my feet,
perhaps one of Aphrodite's golden apples
tossed by Hippomenes as he pursued the swift-footed Atalanta:
    he knew she would stop when she saw it,
      could not resist bending down, reaching for it.
He knew she would not see the trick
until it was too late for her to win the race—
this trick of love that beat her at her own game.

5

At night I lie here on the edge
watching wind blow white caps through Gulf waters.
I remember how we lay together under this same sky,
said the names of stars, told each other their ancient stories—
    the Pleiades riding the back of the bull,
    Cassiopeia rocking, the Great Bear.
In your arms you brought roses
blooming in the moon's light.
You leaned over me then, and I could see beyond
to the beginning of all things.

Reading the Tarot, New York

The setting doesn't really matter,
so let's imagine an empty room.

She waits by the window in a wooden chair,
builds a fire. Autumn gold falls; winter storms
come to shake her; snow blinds.
They appear to her then—the wise old Crone
with shrouded face, the Hierophant
bringing learned books, a circle of Daughters.

It is the time of Nines, the number
of completion, the cycle's end.
She begins to listen—each morning
feeds the cats, spreads butter on toast,
arranges the table with a wine-red napkin,
a fragile plate—her mother's mother's.

She gathers pears from the grocer, coquinas
from the shore, drinks tea from flowered cups
and tends these days as carefully
as she once held her newborn babies.

Before long she hears the summons, looks out.
Something blooms against the sky—
small, green, fragrant, just a fleck of purple.
She reaches out. Holds on.

Still Waters

for Donna Masini

The idea of the river is that which pulls you back.
—*New York Times* review of David Rabb's *Those the River Keep*

Today the river flows through watery fields of saw grass.
No stillness yet, but that will come.
Today, only signs of life destroying itself:
    a plastic bottle cap from a child's thermos,
    a gray sock too shredded to tell its story.
The ducks are there too
and black sinuous bodies of river snakes.

But along about sunset the white heron appears,
wings wide, flying low, a momentary shadow
on the already darkening surface, a weary archangel
come back to haunt the living,
trumpeting a long, mournful mating cry.

Then the river stills, calls forth its stories
of some so weighted with stones
they stayed deep within, of bodies
so split apart they could not rise again.

She wanders to the edge and looks in.
Maybe she touches the water with her finger,
dreams the river holding her, whispering
its secrets in her ears.

But she will not stay,
this woman on the edge
of the river; she will turn now,
walk back up the bank,
snip a summer's rose from the vine,
catch a glimpse of the cardinal's wing,
listen as the moon
rises above this darkened path of cypress and palm,
charting the eastern sky.

Silver Song, a Sapphic Ode

Enter. Green calls now with no dress of comfort.
Weathered palm trees, empty of youthful branches,
glow. A soft fire flickers through dappled pebbles.
Come to the blooming.

Words of new songs wing just as night advances
home, where breasts, hands, longing encircle, startle.
Fingers tease light, play with a lock of copper
hair on her shoulder,

linger, seek gold spirals of spirit dancing.
Seas recede. Sand, amber, and shells now gather.
Fair as a bright sun lighting a sky is she, a
singer of silver.

Bridge Street

I saw you on Bridge Street just last week,
driving away from the Post Office
in your '57 turquoise Thunderbird,
the one you managed to keep alive
despite your mechanic's dire predictions.
Today I read in the paper
you are gone.

I want to spend my last days as you did—dressed
to the nines, wearing a red straw hat
to cover gray hair and shade a deeply lined face,
eating *profiteroles* covered in chocolate sauce
for breakfast at the French Café, driving
the car of my dreams,
not caring what will happen
next week.

Along the Railroad Tracks
(in San Miguel de Allende, Mexico)

I hear that train too, Neal Cassady,
as it whistles in the stillness of these Mexican nights,
tunneling under a sky of blinking stars
past distant lights in the hills,
whistling in harmony with the three sweet chimes
of the Church of San Antonio at 3 am.

I hear it, and I wonder what
you were hearing, what you were searching for
on those tracks
there among the cacti of this dry desert land.

Did those whistles lure like the Sirens
on Odysseus's journey home?
Did they call out—another adventure
just ahead, around the bend?
Did you want to follow
to a new town, a new bottle of tequila, a new woman?

Or was it as simple as a yearning for a childhood
Christmas morning,
the whistle of an imagined miniature train
left under the tree,
your mother's hands?

Or a longing for an old couple
lying somewhere in silence
startled in the quiet hours
by the sound of a creak in the hallway,
hoping perhaps
one of their own
had come home?

Whitehead Street, Key West

Tell me the names of these flowers, you said,
as we walked along Whitehead Street
in the humid August afternoon. So I did.

The yellow vine is Allamanda; the pink
and white fragrant flowers are frangipani
from the East; and those hedges

are double Hibiscus—orange, pink, yellow, white.
High up in the branches, close to heaven,
is the Royal poinciana.

Say it again, you said. Say it slowly.
Spell it. Write it down. *ROYAL POINCIANA*
red—like the highlights glowing in your hair,

the husky sound of your voice,
my cheeks burning in the shadows,
the sunset lingering over the Gulf.

Union Square, late September

Pink delicate roses push their way through the soil under Gandhi's
  bare feet.
Vendors display not-quite-red-tomatoes, pots of mums and garden
  Asters.
Mothers with their strollers don't seem to notice

but this fake finery doesn't fool me.
I saw the man asleep on the subway grate this morning,
staking out his winter home.

Uptown, the city is cloaked. Brown and gray
cover the faces of the homeward-rushing crowds on 57th Street.
Inside the gallery, the bold eyes of Georgia O'Keeffe stare

frozen through the lens of Stieglitz's camera.
They do not speak to me.
On West 23rd Street, late afternoon,

wind forces my hands into empty pockets,
blows ragged handbills around my ankles.
So this is how it feels?

When I reach the river,
I am not surprised
to find dark mist blanketing the view south.

The Descent

God watched the angels fall . . .
—Brigit Peegen Kelly

I

and did nothing to stop them as he sat up high.
Maybe he pushed them out of heaven himself.

The way those angels fell—
white feathers floating on a summer day
becoming dense as they neared earth,
bundles of starched shirts fresh from the laundry.

Out of keeping with autumn's
other colors of amber and green, a hint of purple.
So much white,
strange coming through the heavens like that.

Only an ordinary Tuesday,
yet the heavens were wearing white,
little girls going to First Communion,
nurses in an elevator at the end of the day.

With flutes and mandolins
they sang as they descended:
    glorious *glorias,*
    exalted *Kyrie eleisons.*

Some landed right outside my door.
Others (it was reported) in large city parks and fields of grain.
Confusing traffic signals, they floated to runways,
landed on highways, at shopping malls.

No one welcomed the angels
if they saw them at all,
mistook them for drag queens, gypsies
or other intruders into clear fields of vision.

I I

What kind of name do they give it,
this field where they landed?
A place to get jobs? drink sodas at lunch?
go home to the television's screen?

They push hard against the tide,
try not to forget the descent, try not to forget
that white becoming,
all those floating moments before entry.

It is important to keep moving
against the flow of tourists on 5th Avenue,
the rush into subway tunnels at 5:30,
against the crowd around the linens at Macy's.

It is important to keep moving
else they become still and know they can't remember.

To Persephone

Could you hear your heart beat
when you left that long, dark hall?
Did you trip on the hem of your skirt?

You had no candle to guide you,
only smoking red embers licking
your ankles, your sandal straps.

Did your fingers tremble feeling their way back
to green earth after months underground
serving him wine, your mother's best cherries?

The story says you were ready to return
to fields of corn ripening on amber Sicilian hills,
knowing the March morning, the whole world, in fact,

awaited you with held breath.
But I *have* to know: in that moment
before your eyes met the sun,

before you stepped forth,
did you raise a hand to your brow,
pluck at your crimson-stained gown?

Did you hate the scent of all those flowers?
And did you remember then
the sweet, familiar taste of that ripe fruit on your tongue?

Was it then that you turned?
Was it then that everything in you
wanted to pull back?

Coincidences *(after W. S. Merwin)*

If I had not walked with you to school every morning for the
first six years and if you had not had an aunt who lived in one of
the downstairs bedrooms whose door was right beside the grand
piano where we used to sing *That's My Desire* and *Slow Boat to
China*   if you had not moved to Atlanta leaving me with no
one to share Friday nights   to read forbidden books from the
local library or diaries packed away in old trunks   to dress up in
antique dresses and hats   if I hadn't kissed Jim in the back seat of
the blue '55 Ford one moonlit night   if his brother hadn't gone
away to fight in Korea   come back home to marry my cousin   if
my grandmother hadn't died giving birth to my mother and her
twin sister who were then separated for twelve years to be raised
by maiden aunts   if my father had not continued to live his entire
life in the house on Clark Street where he was born so that we
could never live anywhere else except summers on Kingsley Lake
in a cottage which he finally lost in a poker game

then I would not have found myself in a studio flat on Bank
Street in the Village that year   watching cruise ships on the
Hudson   sending you post cards   I would not have traveled
so far to spend the winter shivering   clinging to the sides of
buildings during nineteen snow storms   walking Village streets
on my way to 7th Avenue   taking the subway to the ferry while
the wind blew icy through the cracks of my ancient room   the
sun set by four   all I could do was wait   with my arms folded
around my knees.

The Nearness of Water

I heard your laugh and turned to take your hand
but I was alone at the edge of sunset
watching a magenta sun slide into the horizon.

> *The winter I left I wrote in the diner on 23rd street.*
> *It was cold. I wore a black velvet hat. I was never*
> *more than a tourist in your wildness. You sent me*
> *postcards with red flowers in the background.*

One night I returned to a place I knew well.
Guided by pink azaleas and pale coquina shells,
I cupped your face with my hand and traced each line,
each eyelash, the tip of your nose, the curve of your ear,
searching for a way back to tangled terrains, to sea oats,
driftwood, cypress knees, sand dollars buried lightly in the surf,
the growing lavender of the sea rose.

> *Solitude is a double rainbow over the Everglades*
> *late afternoon; one bubble from my kitchen sink, sailing across*
>   *the room,*
> *hovering, until it lands in the palm of my hand; opening the*
>   *door*
> *on Friday afternoons into a room without you.*

I would begin again with oak trees and the nearness of water
to learn to make a home for myself—
    a black cat sprawled across my lap, a Schubert sonata,
    a slow rain falling.

On Avenue A *(after Octavio Paz)*

1

The moon inside the night,
    the answer inside the moon
        caressed stars.
My memory curves inward.

Under the cover of night's softness
    I am wavering into palm trees
        of this unsung green.
The light has become your name,

not of words but of stars.
    I cannot enter the glow.
        I cannot breathe.
The past is a yellow buttercup under your chin.

2

I am in a room surrounded by music.
    Carved
        promises enter the notes.
The candle flickers and dims by itself.

The golden light
    through the early morning
        spirals back and forth in my head.
There is white, white.

A great blue heron
    still strolls down the sandy lane.
        I dance with it
when I long for you.

3

The stream is flowing like a tear.
    You are flowing like a poem.
        The light weeps to itself
when it thinks of yesterday.

The light glows
    deeper and deeper
        in your cold eyes.
I am the light you do not hear.

The light through the eyes of night knows what I sing.
    You are in a foreign country,
        nights with no one.
Names of me are hiding.

The Meaning of Yellow Things

1

All day it rained violent gusts from the south.
Later I stood on the deck watching the moon
break through clouds across the bay,
lighting a path to my door.

It felt like that day in April
when I walked 8th Street in the Village
only a week after the last winter storm
and found Forsythia blooming

in a snow-filled corner.
The world begins in such moments—
  pale crystals of moonlight on choppy waters,
  yellow flowers frozen against an iron fence.

2

If all paths lead back to the self
then perhaps the *via regia*
is the sandy lane outside my front door
bordered by oleander and Jacaranda
and other names that sound like love.

3

Some Tuesday morning
in the middle of 5th Avenue
it might be there: Stonehenge maybe
or a grocery cart filled with Tulips.
And right in the middle of life
you change directions.

4

I was running on a beach somewhere
looking at the water meet the edge of the sky like that.
I remembered your hands,
how the horizon curved around us.
Maybe that's the way the end of love feels:
    late afternoon
    red sky blending into still blue waters.

After You Left

After you left,
it was only in that one moment when I woke each morning
did I forget you were gone.
Only then was there an absence of the loss of you.

When you left, all the world stopped
and I had to learn again to make coffee,
tie my shoes,
to wake up and go to sleep.

On the airplane flying south, I learned how cold felt.
I did not know how it would feel to go home
with you not there or how to make a home
for myself under oak trees beside water.

I waited for birds to fly overhead
and even in New York that year
I watched deep red sunsets over the Hudson
and thought of you and made homes.

After you left, I looked at hands on subways, in diners,
stared at the veins,
the way long fingers tapped
or short ones grasped the stem of a glass.

Once (years later) I saw your hands again
lying idly on a table,
the skin where your elbow bends creased like fine parchment
and I remembered how your hands knew,

how they once reached for me—hands
now resting on a table.
I could only look at them.
When you were gone

I rode the current on,
helpless to stop.
I reached out my hand to catch you
but your hands were frozen.

They could not reach back or even wave goodbye.
They let me go alone
to places I never thought I could go
alone, and even now

when lilacs bloom in April, even now
in one distilled moment
I look for you on the shore,
smell lilacs and remember.

Remembering June

Late afternoons you might see the wind
blow across the bay, bending pines
to the earth, dashing waves against rocks
and you might hear thunder
across an open sea, watch lightning flash
behind billowing backs of clouds

Imagine me then, walking
this shore, heavy like the heat, wrapped
in a stillness that has become home, reluctant
to turn away from the fierceness of this August day,
remembering June.

Summer will soon end; it is too late
to walk with you through waveless waters,
too late to retrace our steps
or seek a different shore
for we are as linked as this sea
making clouds making rain.

So imagine me remembering June
and the depths of your eyes.
Invite me in. We have time enough
for small moments—a sonnet perhaps
or an adagio from our favorite sonata.

Letting Go

We were joined
by silk sashes and daisy chains.
We grew light and began to sing—
our hair braided
in the wind and all across our pillows each spinning night.

These are the last ties
to be cut, always the last,
those that gather quietly
    invisible but heavy
like your breath
brushing the back of my neck

Haikus

Bitter persimmons
in a painted copper bowl
the end of passion

My life, a mem'ry,
carved in the shape of your hand
that was yesterday

Simple Things

You begin with simple things,
put one foot in front of the other,
breathe in and out
and soon you find you can wash the dishes,
take out the trash, make the bed.

One morning you might wake up
and see the sun piercing the horizon
while you have a cup of coffee.

It begins to be better
when you can read the morning paper,
pay attention to the evening news,
even balance your checkbook, polish your nails,
remember what you went to the kitchen for.

But if it still takes forever to pull off your boots
or raise that fork of lettuce to your mouth,

you return to simple things—
feed cats, water plants, write your brother,
curl up on the couch with an afghan
pulled up to your neck,
listen to sounds of quietness
in your room

Then one afternoon
    (it **can** *happen)*
you simply get off that couch, put on your coat,
walk out the door
and buy the largest, freshest bagel
in all of New York City.

Rue Mouffetard, early June

I walk uphill past fruit stands—
boxes of raspberries, rows of apricots,
peaches stacked in careful pyramids.

Then, the markets: fresh chickens in a row like tombstones,
baked chickens turning on racks of skewers.
Sparrows perch there when no one is looking.

On the corner is the *chocolatier.*
Wooden paddles churn sticky syrup—
soon to be creams and ganache truffles.

Women click past—smart suits, shoulder pads, stockings with
        seams,
shoes with pointed toes and little sharp heels—
always slender, always carrying straw shopping baskets.

So Parisian—going to market
on this narrow cobblestone street,
the 14th century route from Paris to Rome.

Renoir

When his fingers could no longer move,
when they were petrified by disease,

Renoir strapped brushes to his wrists
and painted—landscapes, crowds of people dancing,

two young women (one blond, one brunette)
their hands slender and pale

lying quite at ease in the folds
of their starched and aproned laps.

from Greece Journal

Another August—
how many left to feel the heat of summer's dog days,
to see goldenrod in ditches beside the road?

Last night the moon passed through the sky
behind a blanket of white clouds.
This morning, no rain again.

We think we're in Dante's Inferno
but it's only August, the last day,
and we're merely passing through.

Poem from Vienna

Today you enter my thoughts
like the opening refrains of a Strauss waltz
from last night's operetta.
If you were here, I would buy you a flower
from the stall on the corner and introduce you
to the kind-faced Viennese gentleman
who sits beside me on the park bench, humming
under his breath to violin sounds from the bandstand.

If you were here, I would take you to the café
where I have *Kaffee mit Milch* every afternoon
served by the smiling, blond-haired waitress
who always brings, unasked, a glass of cold water
and tells me *Auf Wiedersehen* when I leave.

If you were here, I would be
as the alpine flowers I see from the train window,
thriving on the mountainside
where they belong.

Night Train Through France

On my first train trip through the Alps,
from Luxembourg to Rome,
we were young with our backpacks,
recited Millay and cummings,
sometimes Eliot's lines about journeys—
the way we always arrive where we started
and know the place for the first time.

I rode through France on a wooden bench, third class,
sitting up all night in a compartment
with a young father and son who spoke only French.
All we could do
was watch together the white snows of the Alps
under the light of a full moon,
quiet, until the boy reached in his bag
for a wrapped chocolate—sticky and smashed
from so much traveling—placed it in my palm
softly, the way a kitten can edge its way
to the hem of your skirt, then,
lying on its back, bat it with white paws
until you have to stop, scoop it up,
let it sleep in your lap while you read.

Perhaps Edna Millay took this same trip through the Alps,
riding all night the way she rode the ferry
back and forth, laughing and merry.
In the morning she gave a bag of peaches and all her coins
to an old woman at the station.
Perhaps she would have spoken French
to the young boy
had a gift for him in her bag—a miniature of the Eiffel Tower
or a souvenir spoon with the Alps carved in the handle.

Madrid Moments

If I were to write of a moment in Madrid, it would have to be the way the early morning sun shone through the heavy wooden shutters in my room at *Chaminade,* making egg-shaped patterns on the wall and across my face. Or it might tell of the Silversmith at his booth at the *El Rasto* market, who replied, *Are you rich or are you poor?* when I asked the price of a silver bracelet.

Maybe a Madrid moment happened one late afternoon when I saw Georgia O'Keefe's *A Street in New York* and the orange tree in Lope de Vega's courtyard, both so familiar yet so very far from home. Or another time at the *Plaza del Mayor* with *churros y chocolate* as a blue moon slid across the clear night sky and gypsies played *Ave Maria* in the open square.

A Madrid moment might have in it the laughter of the young people in the disco across the street every morning at 4:30, or eating dinner at 10:00 pm, or walking uphill past bushes of lavender to go anywhere, and how all that began to seem normal. Then again, I should not leave out the half moon hanging low in the sky over a cobblestone courtyard as we watched *Flamenco* surrounded by massive iron gates and crumbling brick walls with no windows—centuries of monarchy being mocked by the sound of shoes with a hundred nails and throaty voices singing like moans of young lovers or the loss of dreams.

And I must include the magic of seeing Goya's *black paintings* on a day when fuchsia flowers hung in baskets around the entrance to *El Prado* or standing for the first time in front of

Picasso's *Guernica* for as long as I wanted, then strawberry ices in the garden.

But the most magic of Madrid moments happened only after I closed the door to Room 302, closed the door to the small pot of mums still sitting on the desk, said good by to the tree outside the window where an occasional magpie will ever join the chattering sparrows, when I closed the door on the city of blue skies and leafy green boulevards, and, without postcards or photographs, Madrid became my own.

On Viewing Henri Cartier-Bresson's Photograph, *Seville, Espagne, 1933*

The morning after the revolution, children taunt
a boy on crutches who hobbles away from the scene
into the camera's field of vision.

There is nowhere left to go,
only this hole in the wall and rubble covering the ground
where a row of houses once stood.

Perhaps the boy on crutches lived here, or these bullies.
Perhaps only last night in this very spot a family sat down for a
    meal,
forks poised as the food was being blessed,

the children's pink tongues licking
as they waited for their grandmother's *paella.*
Only last night someone's little sister sat in her high chair

there in the corner where today the broken stones form a small
    mound.
Did she wave her fork in the air to imitate her brothers
who were busy anticipating the taste of yellow rice

steaming with pieces of fish and sausage, red wine,
fist-sized wedges of bread? Now there is rubble
so they chase the boy on crutches, the helpless one.

Perhaps it had been his father who had led a group of soldiers
to this spot where the family was eating.
Maybe they were pursuing their neighbor, a spy

who gave away secrets. Perhaps it had been his father
giving the orders to shoot at this kitchen where someone's
family sat listening to the blessing of the food,

smelling the saffron that permeated the small room.
Or perhaps the boy's father had been home sleeping.
It doesn't matter. All that is left is a hole in the wall

to mark a couple's bedroom where she gave birth to five children.
He would pin her thighs in a desperate embrace then slap her;
his passion was so great.

The bedroom is rubble
so is the street where the row of houses stood only yesterday.
The children chase this boy, taunt him, toss bits of stone

or the broken arm of a porcelain doll
some young wife brought with her to Seville
from the mountains of Andalusia on her wedding day.

In the photograph, a young girl laughs and raises her skirt in an
    obscene gesture;
a young mother with a bucket seeks water or food
to feed what family she has left.

The boy on crutches has nowhere to go, no path, no alley
no small hope of escape. He will be caught.
He moves directly into the line of the camera.

Sirens

The breeze
    released purple longing
        from inside wet rain

then danced
    soft as a hummingbird
        and held on, quickened

breathless
    in search of silver song,
        fragrant as Freesia.

Postcards from Tuscany

I sent ten postcards today
>   to say *I wish you   were here*
>>   to see the sun shine sepia

over terra cotta roofed villages.
>   Poets write of the *bliss of solitude,*
>>   but here there is no bliss.

Even the butterflies travel in pairs
>   and the only green hides under the dust
>>   on olive leaves at the foot of the path.

In the noon sun women hang clothes on a line
>   carefully, edge to edge,
>>   one pin for two corners.

Last night, in the middle of *Piazza del Duomo*
>   I thought I heard your laugh
>>   but it was lovers embracing

against the stone walls of the *Campo.*
>   I spend long days wandering up steep hills
>>   along curved alleys, cobblestone paths,

visit churches to see relics—
    St. Catherine's head,
        St. Christopher's cane,

hear strains of *Ave Maria*
    escaping from the door
        of Dante's church.

Yesterday I drank Chianti at a sidewalk café,
    watched brown-haired men with sun-tanned arms
        play chess blindfolded.

Variations on Lines by John Yau, a Pantoum

for Dionisio Martinez

Leonardo knew the wings of birds would one day be worn by men
that they were destined to lift their shadows above the clouds.
—John Yau

One day men would wear wings.
Leonardo knew this
but he did not know what would happen to women
when men used the wings of birds to rise above clouds.

Leonardo didn't know this.
Women would wave goodbye and plant seeds
when men used the wings of birds to rise above clouds.
They would build Maypoles in spring and garnish them with
flowers.

Women waved goodbye and planted seeds
in fields next to flocks of white sheep and brown cows.
They built Maypoles in spring and garnished them with flowers,
glancing occasionally at shadows flying overhead.

In fields next to flocks of white sheep and brown cows
women grew deep into dark earth.
While glancing occasionally at shadows flying overhead
they buried the dead and planted potatoes.

Women grew deep into dark earth
when men grew wings to fly overhead.
They buried the dead and planted potatoes
and filled front porches with rocking chairs, lemonade, jump
    ropes.

When men grew wings to fly overhead
women grew roses on lattice fences,
filled front porches with rocking chairs, lemonade, jump ropes
and walked with shoulders high toward each other.

Women grew roses on lattice fences
while men were destined to lift their shadows above the clouds.
Women walked with shoulders high toward each other
and forgot about the wings of birds worn by men.

Men were destined to lift their shadows above the clouds
but they didn't know what happened to women.
All Leonardo knew was
one day men would wear wings.

The Stardust Mission

Scientists
search the universe for signs of the origin of life,
wait on a remote stretch of salt flat in the Utah desert

scanning the sky for the *Stardust* space capsule
bringing data buried in the ice and debris
of a 4.5 million year old comet.

They probe ferns in dark holes of interstellar swamps,
dredge the icy dark of Antarctic waters,
inspect living cells of proteins and peer into pre-biotic soup.

We are born of stardust, they conclude.
We are the children of dust
radiating from stars swirling through the atmosphere.

But I don't need a scientist to tell me
I'm a child of stardust.
The origin of my life begins at home.

The ancient memory of flowing through space
ignites when I see moss hanging from oak trees
gleaming like handmade lace veils on a moonlit night,

watch lightning jewel the night sky behind a bamboo hedge,
drink Prosecco in the front yard on Mother's Day,
see the green phosphorus flash at the top of a wave

crashing on the white sand of my island home.
Or when my grandsons fall asleep
before I finish the first chapter

of a Harry Potter novel. Long before
we reach the part where the cat is reading the street sign,
their little eyes blink and flicker and finally close

and for a moment we're united,
a sparkling tableau—
the children of stardust.

The Storyteller *(after Walt Whitman)*

Little George asked, Where is my story? bringing me his book at
    the end of the day.
I wanted to read him the story of his life . . . but I do not even
    know one for my own life.
I guess stories might be like the waves we bounce over, on our way
    to the sand bar just off shore.

Or they might be quilts, hand stitched from threads of train
    whistles, butterfly wings, black river stones.
Maybe words printed on a white linen page,
    lies told around campfires then chiseled by muddy, blood-
    stained fingers on cave walls lit by a single flame.

Slowly I will tell you my favorite tale
and you may make it your own.
If I write it myself it will have wings
    and will be about a hero or a small rabbit
    or a child herself
to be placed in the hands of this other child.

Some stories are too dark for this little boy,
darker than his room at night or the blue under his eyelids
    when he closes his eyes,
dark enough to make him reach for a touch.

Stories are still here and there,
        powerful words that stay alive.
And if they never were, there can really be no living.
And if they are, there can be no death
        waiting at The End
to stop the breath when the last word is said.

All is said and sung, and everything matters.
And to be the Storyteller is different from what anyone supposes.
They are chosen to bear the weight of dark hours and bursts of
        light.

Mary Katherine Wainwright is a retired professor of American literature currently living in San Miguel de Allende, Mexico. She earned her Ph.D. in American Studies at Purdue University, and taught literature and writing for over thirty years in major U.S. colleges and universities, including State College of Florida, Eckerd College, College of Staten Island, and the University of South Florida.

Wainwright has received numerous fellowships and awards from the National Endowment for the Humanities and the McKnight Foundation for Higher Education, among others, and her poetry and prose have been published in many literary journals, including *Kalliope, Phoebe, Solemente en San Miguel II, Florida English,* and *Sarasota Review. A Taste of Salt* is her first published collection of poetry.

34648603R00050

Made in the USA
Columbia, SC
16 November 2018